Jane's GUIDE TO Dicks

(AND Toms AND Harrys)

Ross & Kathryn Petras

Andrews McMeel
Publishing, LLC
Kansas City • Sydney • London

Andrews McMeel Publishing, LLC
an Andrews McMeel Universal company
1130 Walnut Street, Kansas City, Missouri 64106

www.andrewsmcmeel.com

11 12 13 14 15 TEN 10 9 8 7 6 5 4 3 2 1

ISBN: 978-1-4494-0157-3

Library of Congress Control Number: 2010930614

Book design by Holly Ogden

ATTENTION: SCHOOLS AND BUSINESSES
Andrews McMeel books are available at quantity discounts with bulk purchase for educational, business, or sales promotional use. For information, please e-mail the Andrews McMeel Publishing Special Sales Department: specialsales@amuniversal.com

Jane's GUIDE TO Dicks

Other books from Ross and Kathryn Petras

B Is for Botox

1, 2, Can't Reach My Shoe

This is *Jane*.

This is her boyfriend, *Dick*.

Once upon a time, Jane was clueless about Dick.

She liked him, but she couldn't make him notice her.

She didn't know how to talk to him. She didn't know how to act on a date. She didn't know when to say yes and when to say no.

 Jane says:

"In other words, I didn't know Jack about Dick!"

Ha ha, Jane! That is funny. But it is also very true.

Of course, now Jane and Dick are *likethis*. So how did she do it? What are Jane's special secrets?

She is going to share them with you—so you can get your OWN Dick!

(Or Tom. Or Harry.)

Now let's get started.

The Basic Boy

Jane's Special Secret #1:
Take the time to *study* boys.

We all know that boys are very different from girls. So sometimes it is hard for girls to know how to act.

But you can't know how to act if you don't know how boys *think*. And *thinking* is what (sometimes) happens in the "boy brain."

Yes, boys have brains too! But just like boys have different "plumbing" than girls, they have different brains as well. It's just that you can't see the difference because boy brains don't stick out like those other things boys have.

Let's talk to our good friend Dr. Felix. Dr. Felix is a special kind of doctor called a "psychiatrist." That means that he is an expert on brains. He will be able to tell us a great deal about boy brains.

Dr. Felix

Here is his scientific diagram of the boy brain.

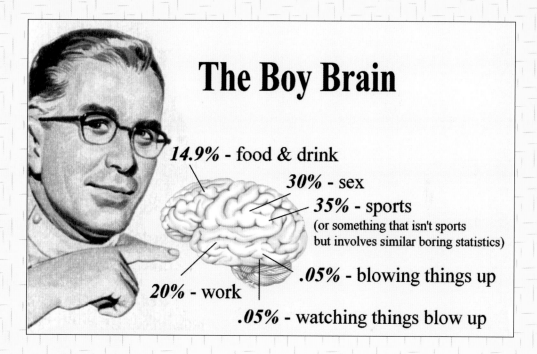

The Boy Brain

14.9% - food & drink

30% - sex

35% - sports
(or something that isn't sports
but involves similar boring statistics)

.05% - blowing things up

20% - work

.05% - watching things blow up

Are boy brains different from girl brains, Dr. Felix?

"Indeed they are. For one thing, girls rarely think about blowing things up. But there's also a great deal more."

Let's take a look inside two brains on a movie date. Both brains are processing the film on the screen. It is a romantic film about an airplane pilot and a nurse.

The girl brain is thinking:

This film reminds me of my relationship with Ted. I think we're moving on to another level. I hope so. I really think we're sympathetic souls. I wonder what he's thinking right now . . .

The boy brain is thinking:

Wow, those sure sound like different brains, Dr. Felix!

"Yes, extremely so," explains Dr. Felix. "The girl brain is:

  (1) analytical;
  (2) sensitive;
  (3) intellectually questing;
  (4) other-oriented.

The boy brain is:

  (1) happily uncomplicated;
  (2) sex-/food-oriented."

Gee, the boy brain sounds kind of like a dog's, doesn't it?

"Hmm," says Dr. Felix. "Or should I say 'arf'?"

Jane's Special Secret #1: A Real-Life Example

Sarah could never get the courage to talk to handsome Van. "He's so hot. And so deep! I never know what to say to him!" Yes. Sarah suffered from a lack of confidence.

Sarah, tongue-tied and awkward with boys

Then Sarah learned all about the boy brain—and how it is almost exactly like a dog brain. "Hey," thought Sarah, "if I picture him looking like sweet, cuddly Scamp, maybe I won't be tongue-tied when I talk to him."

Sarah, confident due to Dog Visualization Technique

Sarah picked her childhood cocker spaniel—and it worked wonders!

What kind of dog would YOU pick?

Jane says:

"Visualize that special boy as a dog, and your confidence problems are over!"

Jane's Special Secret #2:

Sometimes YOU just shouldn't be that into THEM—or them into you. So to speak.

Yes. Not all boys are created equal. Literally.

For example, you may have noticed that boys have different sized . . . *machines.*

Some of them have BIG machines.

Big

And some of them have SMALL machines.

Small

And some of them have MEDIUM-SIZED machines.

Medium

Each one of them says that his machine is JUST THE RIGHT size.

That is not true.

Here is a question for you: If you wanted to mow an acre, would you rather use a ride-on mower? Or a push mower?

 Jane says:
"No matter what anyone tells you, a BIG machine is usually BETTER!"

 Jane adds:
"But not TOO big!"

Jane's Special Secret #3:

We have looked at the boy brain and talked about the boy machine. There is another part of boys that you should know about. Boys' eyes.

Does Jane mean whether a boy has blue or brown eyes?

No. She does not mean eye color. She means something else. But what could that be?

Let us talk to Dr. Felix again. "Why should a girl have to know anything about boys' eyes, Dr. Felix?"

"Hmmm," says Dr. Felix. "Well, in many cases, a boy's optic nerve is connected directly to his crotch."

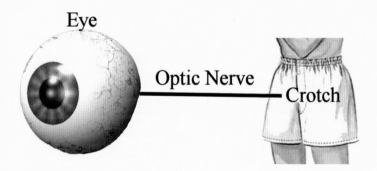

This means that the nerve in some boys' eyes that makes them able to see is—well, connected directly "down below." And *this* means that those boys see things *very* differently than girls.

This can be a problem on dates.

Jane's Special Secret #3: A Real-Life Example

Look at Tiffany and Tim. They are having an all-too-typical boy-girl conversation.

See?

Tiffany is talking to Tim's face. And Tim is talking to Tiffany's chest.

Do chests have ears, Tim?

"Uh . . . no, I guess," says Tim. "But they sure look good!"

 Jane says:

"Boys who forget you have a face are the *real* boobs!"

So You Want to Date a Boy . . .

Okay, so we have learned a little bit about the biology of boys and what makes them "tick." Now your next step is to make your target Dick "tick" for you—and that means . . . dating!

Jane's Special Secret #4:

Before you date, be sure you are READY to date a boy.

Are you?

It is a good idea to be honest with yourself. Start by asking yourself: What is your attitude toward people of the male persuasion?

This is very important when you are figuring out if you really are ready.

For example, here is someone who is probably not ready to date:

Men are nicotine-soaked, beer-besmirched, whiskey-greased, red-eyed devils.

And here is someone who is probably ready to date.

real estate agent who is showing Amy apartments

Amy

APARTMENT FOR

To be absolutely sure whether it's time for *you* to "dive into the dating pool," take this specially designed standardized test. Note: You will need a No. 2 pencil (sharpened). Fill in the oval corresponding to your answer. Maximum test-taking time is thirty (30) minutes. When you have completed the test, consult the answer key at the bottom of the page. (Don't peek! And remember—there are no right or wrong answers.*)

(*Except for #3.)

Standardized Dick Dating Readiness Test
(SDDRT)

1) I am 13 or older.   True ○   False ○

2) I like boys.   True ○   False ○

3) A beam of particles of charge $q = 5 \cdot 10\text{-}20$ C and mass $m = 2 \cdot 10\text{-}25$ kg enters an area with a magnetic field of magnitude $B = .2$T with a speed of 103 m/s. The path of the particles is a circular arc of radius R. The gravitational force is negligible. Radius R would then be .02m.   True ○   False ○

SDDRT *Answer Key:* If you answered TRUE to questions 1 and 2, yes, you are ready for dating.
If you also answered TRUE to question 3, you are not only ready for dating, you are ready for an advanced physics course. Congratulations!

Jane's Special Secret #5:

**The most important thing to keep in mind:
The "dating game" is a lot like an African safari
(without the Masai warriors. Usually).**

Boys like the thrill of the chase. They like to feel that they have achieved something when they catch a girl. In other words, the boy is the HUNTER. And you, the girl, are the HUNTED—or, more technically, the "prey."

Jane adds:

"And you are 'preying' to be caught!"

Ha ha! Good joke, Jane. But let us be serious. How do you get a boy to chase you and, eventually, catch you? It's simple:

You have to be the right kind of prey!

Let us discuss this with top TV wildlife personality (and best-selling author) Earl Duke.

**TV's Top Wildlife Expert Earl Duke
official press photograph**

He goes on safari often and dates a lot too, so he can tell you how to attract the hunter with the biggest gun!

What kind of prey (girls) do hunters (boys) prefer, Mr. Duke?

"Off the bat, I'd say lionesses. Every hunter would love to bag a queen of the jungle." (Note: Lionesses = supermodels, top Hollywood actresses, etc.)

But we all can't be lionesses, Mr. Duke!

"Heh heh. You are right. But if you talk with enough hunters, as I have in my role as a TV wildlife personality (and best-selling author), you will discover that hunters often don't actually bag those lionesses. The lionesses are too hard to get."

So what do hunters do? "They seek out the slightly easier target: The fairly obtainable-but-still-hard-to-catch gazelle."

(Note: Gazelles = good-looking girls next door, at the next desk, or across the street—in other words, you!)

Are most girls gazelles, Mr. Duke?

"Oh, no, no! Ha ha! Some girls are antelopes. And that's a darn shame." Why? "No hunter respects an antelope. They're just too easy."

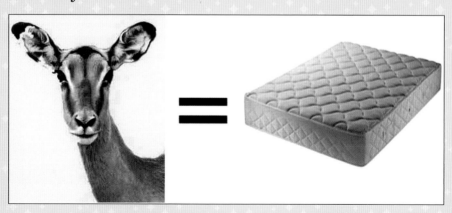

Jane says:

"So, girls, if you're not a lioness, you had better be sure you're a gazelle. Just follow my handy checklist!"

Gazelle Characteristics	How You Can Apply Gazelle Characteristics to Self
Healthful diet	Not too many calories or trans fats. And remember: Gazelles NEVER overdo the processed foods!
Vary their diet according to season	Good idea! Eat lighter in the summer—bikini season!
Sleek, shiny coat	Keep up with those hair appointments. Shampoo daily if needed, and condition, condition, condition!
Eye-catching horns	Accessorize! (Jewelry, scarves, etc. can really enhance your looks!)
Gregarious; forms groupings of small herds of females	It's so much easier to meet a boy when you have a few (but not too many) wingmen (or rather winggirls) with you!
Broad white patch on the rump	Optional

Jane's Special Secret #6:

It's one thing to make yourself the perfect prey, but sometimes your hunter doesn't seem to be carrying the right ammo. (Or *any* ammo, for that matter!)

Yes, it's the sad truth. Some "hunters" are really bad at it (hunting). In fact, they're so bad that you start wondering if they're interested in hunting at all.

We're not saying they're "switch-hitters" (to mix metaphors). But they're just not quick off the mark (to mix more metaphors). In other words, they're shy.

The big question: How do you get these shy guys from Point A (interested in you but doing nothing) to Point B (interested in you and doing something)?

DESIRED ACTION

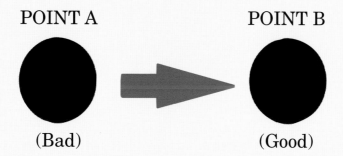

POINT A   POINT B

(Bad)   (Good)

The problem when getting a boy to move from Point A to Point B in relation to you (the girl) is that there is often a very thick wall separating the two of you. This is *literally* a thick wall of negative energy. Its technical name is "the Wall of Male Shyness."

Let us visualize the problem to better understand it—and to explain how you can get past this wall.

THE PROBLEM:

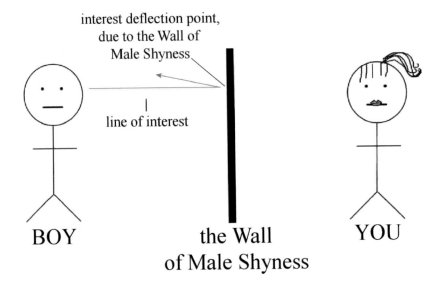

interest deflection point,
due to the Wall of
Male Shyness

line of interest

BOY   the Wall   YOU
of Male Shyness

As you can see, the boy's interest in you is not getting through. It is blocked—or *deflected*—by the wall.

So what can be done?

It is all up to you. *You* will have to break through the Wall of Male Shyness to allow his line of interest to "penetrate" you. (So to speak.)

How?

By using your built-in, superior-to-the-male, female communication skills, of course! You will smash a hole in the Wall of Male Shyness with what we call your "Club of Communication."

Club of Communication

Now let's see that club in action . . .

THE SOLUTION:

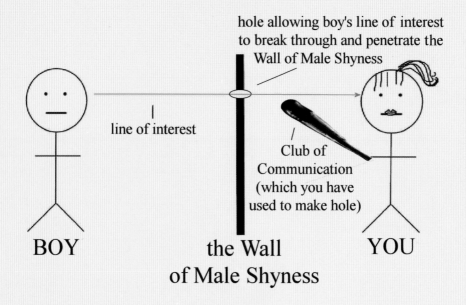

hole allowing boy's line of interest
to break through and penetrate the
Wall of Male Shyness

line of interest

Club of
Communication
(which you have
used to make hole)

BOY

the Wall
of Male Shyness

YOU

Jane says:

"Did you see the added bonus? Notice that
the Wall of Male Shyness isn't *totally* broken
down. Most of it stays up—so he can't reach
OTHER girls with his line of interest. Just
you. He's all yours!"

There are many different kinds of Clubs of Communication you can use. You can use a "club of calling him directly," a "club of asking him out yourself," a "club of walking right over and asking him to dance," and so on. Use whatever "club" you think will work best!

It doesn't really matter what kind of club you use, as long as you get that club and start bashing!

 Jane says:

"In other words, get in touch with your inner cavegirl!"

Jane's Special Secret #7:

Embracing your inner cavegirl is all fine and dandy but—hold on a second—where do you find that perfect caveboy? Simple—you've got to go where the boys are . . . and the girls aren't!

Be creative! Forget the local bar scene—packed with *so* much competition. And how about finding a guy at work? Face it, every other girl is fantasizing about the hot suit in the corner office.

See what we mean?

To get your own Dick, you have to start thinking *outside* the box.

And that's where Jane can help—with her "Best Low Competition High Success Rate Man Haunts Hints." (They've got a great male/YOU ratio!)

 Jane says:

"Try the local rock quarry!"

JANE'S HINT #1:
A Real-Life Example

Mandee:
met foreman Frank at
nearby open pit mine;
now dating exclusively

hydraulic
power
drill

Jane says:

"If you like swimming, find out where an underwater demolition team will be working!"

JANE'S HINT #2: A Real-Life Example

starfish

Chelsea:
swimming next to her guy
ex-Navy SEAL Marcus —
whom she first met at
a depth of 25 feet;
yesterday, he gave her
a natural pearl
pre-engagement ring.

Jane says:

"Polar expeditions are always top-heavy with eligible brainy (and brawny!) scientific he-men! (Plus chilly nights are perfect for cuddling!)"

JANE'S HINT #3:
A Real-Life Example

weather balloon

handsome explorer
Don West: proposed
to Cheryl but
was turned down.

Cheryl:
showing us her scientific hunk
(and fiancé) astrophysicist
Dr. Schuyler F. Grayson;
has sent out "Save the Date"
cards postmarked South Pole.

Jane says:

"Remember, these are just a few suggestions. There are lots of other Low Competition High Success Rate Man Haunts out there. Just let your imagination run wild! A sewage treatment plant? A rodeo? Give it a whirl!"

Jane's Do's and Don'ts of Successful Dating

It is one thing to date. It is another thing to date WELL.

What do you do on a date? Should you drink too much? (Hint: No.) Should you dress like a slut? (Hint: Maybe.)

Jane has collected some of the most important dating Do's and Don'ts to help you in your quest for Dick (or Tom. Or, for that matter, Harry). With these Do's and Don'ts, you will WIN the dating game.

Jane's Special Secret #8:

DO be a biology babe! In other words, use science to tell if he's interested— or if you're just wasting your time.

Yes, biology can be your best buddy!

Boys, like other male mammals, show certain *biological signs* when they are interested in you.

No, not the one you might be thinking of . . .

Jane says:
"Although that is a definite sign that he is interested!"

There are *other* physical signs of interest that can help you figure out if he likes you. You will learn what they are on the next page. But first take this little test to see if you're already a biology babe.

Here are two photographs. They show the same boy in two different situations. In one of these pictures, he is interested in you. In the other picture, he is not.

Can you tell which picture shows the interested boy?

Photograph #1   Photograph #2

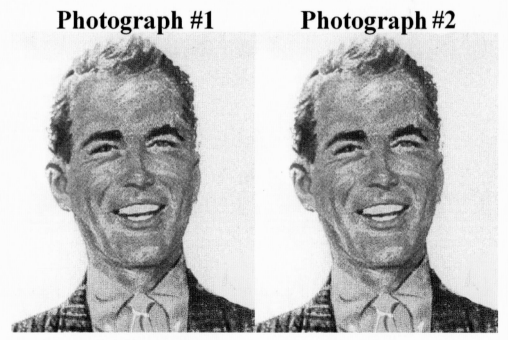

(Do not look at the next page. Don't cheat!)

If you picked picture #1, you are wrong. This boy is NOT interested in you. He is NOT dating material.

Notice the telltale biological features of noninterest:

Photograph #1

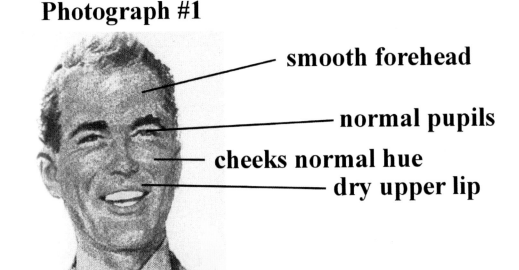

— smooth forehead

— normal pupils

— cheeks normal hue

— dry upper lip

— tie tied normally

If you picked picture #2, congratulations! You won't go wrong with this one. Date this boy and soon! As you can see below, he has all of the telltale biological features of interest.

Photograph #2

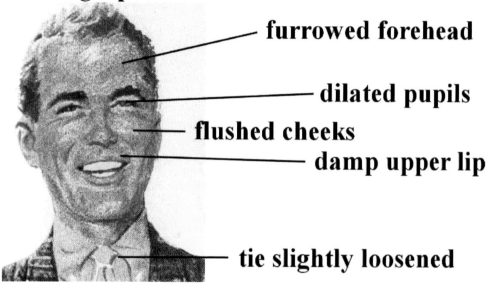

— furrowed forehead

— dilated pupils

— flushed cheeks

— damp upper lip

— tie slightly loosened

Jane says:

"Wasn't that easy! And so educational!"

Jane's Special Secret #8: A Real-Life Example

Some girls take science a step further when it comes to meeting men. Like Courtney the chemistry whiz.

Courtney was sick and tired of the bar scene and all that competition. Too many girls. Too few eligible boys. A lot of lonely Saturday nights. A lot of Chunky Monkey and HBO.

So Courtney decided to do something about it.

She took a few science courses and learned the art of chemical attraction. More important, she learned about sex pheromones—the special chemicals people secrete to attract mates.

"This gives me an idea," thought the chemically creative Courtney.

Yes, as you may have guessed, after weeks of intensive experimentation, Courtney succeeded in making her own special "cologne" of sex pheromones. Now boys are swarming around her like flies around a pile of steaming . . . wait. No. Bad analogy.

But you get the idea, don't you?

 Jane says:

"Thanks to modern science, Courtney's love life has gone from blah to ta-da!"

Jane's Special Secret #9:

DO make the perfect first impression by learning what boys look for in a girl.

A good first impression leads to a good second impression, which leads to a good third impression. Do you see the pattern?

Yes, a good first impression leads to good later things.

Maybe even marriage! (If that's what you want.) This is why it is important to know all the little things you can do to make that first impression as fabulous as you are.

The trick is *knowing what attracts boys in those first important minutes*.

So let's turn the tables and ask *Dick* for his very special masculine insights about making a fabulous first impression.

Dick, what should a girl do?

(1) Smell good.

Dick says: "When a girl smells bad, it's really a turn off."

(2) Look good.

Dick says: "I like girls that look good. Ones that look bad aren't as appealing to me."

(3) Have a good personality.

Dick says: "I like it a lot when a girl has a good personality."

(4) Be a good conversationalist.

Dick says: "I'm really attracted to girls who can think of things to say, especially when I can't think of things to say."

(5) Have a good sense of humor.

Dick says: "Humor is important."

(6) Don't forget to smile.

Dick says: "Smiling is important too."

Wow. Wasn't it interesting and helpful to get inside a boy's complex mind? Thanks a lot, Dick!

Megan Makes the Perfect First Impression

Jane's Special Secret #10:
DON'T get too happy during happy hour !

When you're just starting with a prospect, this is a surefire way to blow it.

Instead of explaining this in detail, let's go to the local pub with Dave and Lauren and see what actually happens. Lauren thinks Dave is cute. She has finally gotten him alone in conversation and he is telling her about himself and his job. Now let's listen in . . .

Here is their conversation after Lauren has had one (1) mojito:

DAVE: "All in all, my job is pretty interesting. But what about you?"

LAUREN: "First I'd love to hear more about you and that absolutely fascinating job of yours!"

[Note: The sober Lauren is able to keep the conversation on the male. This, of course, flatters him and makes her appear even more appealing to him.]

DAVE (thinking): "Wow! She's great! I'm going to ask her out for a series of dates that may very well culminate in a long-term commitment."

[Note: *This is a paraphrase of Dave's* unconscious *thoughts.*]

Visual Depiction of Lauren/Dave Dialogue with One (1) Mojito

Don't the couple look happy?

Now what happens if Lauren has a little more than one mojito? Let's listen in again and find out !

Here is Lauren and Dave's conversation after Lauren has had *five* *(5)* mojitos (in one hour):

DAVE: "All in all, my job *is* pre—"

LAUREN: "Really? My job shucksh. Itsh sho boring. (pause) Wow, theesh mohicans are yummo. I jush hope they're not too fattening since I feel like a blob. I'm all bloated becaush my period ish due and—uh-oh, I don't feel so good . . ."

[Note: *The drunk Lauren is (1) slurring—which sounds unappealing; (2) complaining—which turns boys off; (3) talking about her weight AND her "female" system—which is somewhat off-putting.*]

DAVE (thinking): "Wow! She's bombed! She's plastered. She's toasted. And she's, she's . . . she's blowing chunks! On my foot!"

[Note: *This is a paraphrase of Dave's conscious thoughts.*]

Visual Depiction of Lauren/Dave Dialogue after Five (5) Mojitos

frontal lobe
(attempting to make sense of slurred words)

5 drinks
(chugged)

vomit on shoe
(out of frame)

Doesn't Dave look unhappy?

 Jane says:
"Projectile vomiting is a definite no-no!"*

*(Dick adds: "Especially on suede shoes!")

Jane's Special Secret #11:

DO learn how to fake it.

No, not *that* kind of faking it.

Jane says:

"Although it sure can come in handy!"

We are talking about a different kind of faking it. The kind of faking we are talking about is called *"dull-male-conversation-interest-faking."* If you learn to do it well, it works wonders. Plus you get to keep all of your clothes on! (If you want . . .)

Here are two scientific charts comparing boy talk to girl talk.

First, boy talk:

Average Boy Conversation
Dullness Level Measurements

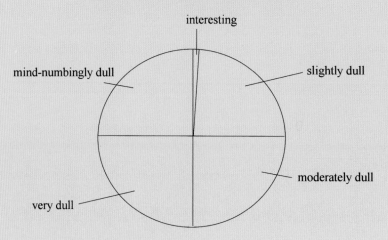

interesting

mind-numbingly dull

slightly dull

moderately dull

very dull

And now, girl talk:

Average Girl Conversation
Dullness Level Measurements

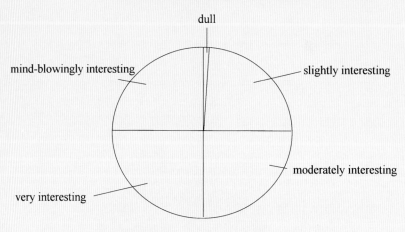

dull

mind-blowingly interesting

slightly interesting

moderately interesting

very interesting

Notice how boring boy conversation is compared to girl conversation. Boy conversation is over 99 percent dull. This is why it is vital to learn how to act interested even if you are ready to fall asleep.

 Jane says:

"Look, kiddos, if you can fake an orgasm—and you know you can!—you can definitely fake an interest in football rushing-yard stats for an hour or two."

Jane is right. This faking technique is very easy. Unlike the other kind of faking it, you don't have to groan. Or scream. Or writhe. All you have to do is put your brain on autopilot, think about anything you want, and say one or two "special words" every few minutes that make it seem like you really care.

To give you an idea of how to do it, here are some real-life examples of boring male conversations and actual replies by girls using Jane's simple technique.

What He Said	What She Said
"So he said that he was a restricted free agent who has been designated as a franchise player and I said no, you idiot. It's been FIVE accrued seasons. That's why MY fantasy football team is so far ahead of his."	"Wow!"
"So I set the straddle up on Mr. Softy at 43 strike. I mean, if anyone bothered to look at the VIX . . ."	"Right!"
"If the manager would just bat him second, I mean, look at his on-base percentage, it's .430 this year, last year it was, what, .395 I think, and, oh yeah, his stealing record . . ."	"Yeah!"
"Then I thought, wait, if I put an E *minor* chord in there. But then I thought, no. Wait. A D7. A *fucking D7!* But THEN I thought . . ."	"Gee!"

Some other "special words" you may want to add to your conversation-with-boy personal database:

Really?	Whoa!
Awesome!	Gosh!
Ohmigod!	That's something!
Sheesh!	Great!
Amazing!	You DID?

Jane says:

"Don't worry—later, when you know it's a serious relationship, you can tell him to shut up!"

Image labels: Chuck; Chuck's fishing rod; salmon; Chuck's other rod

Jane's Special Secret #11: A Real-Life Example

"I am tired of hookups," says Cara. "I want a REAL relationship!" So when she meets Chuck at the local bar, she decides to fake it like a pro. She listens to all of his boring fishing stories.

Like the time he caught the twenty-five-pound chinook salmon.

"Wow," says Cara.

And the time he caught that forty-five-pound channel cat.

"Awesome," says Cara.

"Not to mention the forty-eight-pound grouper ("Ohmigod!"), the thirty-pound coho salmon ("Amazing!"), and the fourteen-pound sockeye ("That's really something!")."

Chuck takes the bait. "Say," Chuck says, "you're the first girl I've met who is actually *interested* in all my fishing stories.

Hey, you know? Maybe we should cast a few lines one of these days."

"Great!"

Now Cara and Chuck have a relationship. Here they are on one of their fishing trips. Cara has just hooked a seven-pound salmon (sockeye). Even better, Cara has hooked a 182-pound Chuck (male).

 Jane says:
"Remember, girls, salmon spawn upstream!"

Jane's Special Secret #12:

Yes, fake it (at the right times), but DO be yourself.

Faking interest in boy conversation is one thing, faking your entire personality is another. If you're fake, then he's fake, then your entire relationship is fake, then what do you have?

Our answer: Not much.

Our advice: Be real.

 Jane says:

"Of course, you can still be real with a push-up bra, a Brazilian, a spray-on tan, and so forth. There IS a limit to reality, n'est-ce pas?"

So when you're on a date, don't pretend to be what you're not. This can cause problems.

Like what happened with Erika . . .

REALLY CUTE GUY: "Are you into extreme sports?"

ERIKA (LYING LIKE CRAZY): "*Am* I?!? The extremer the better!"

And faking it worked . . . kind of. Really Cute Guy asked Erika out on a date, all right. But there's a lesson in this. What happened next? See the next page for the outcome . . .

Erika's *Extremely* Bad Date the Next Week

Jane's Special Secret #13:

DO pick the right time to start having sex with that certain guy.

Jane is asked many questions about sex. Here, plucked from her mailbag, is the question she is asked most often. You've probably asked it yourself—and, at last, you can get an expert answer.

Dear Jane,

Tom and I have been dating for a while now. He wants to start having sex, but I don't know if I'm ready. I'm not sure if I'm serious enough. Is there a *right* time to have sex?

Signed, Confused

Dear Confused,

Yes. There is a right time to have sex. Between 10 P.M. and 1 A.M.

—Jane

Okay, now that Jane has answered that all-important question, let's talk about getting the show on the road.

Sometimes you have to give the boy signals that you are ready to have sex. Taking your clothes off usually works . . . but what if you're on the bus? It's probably not a good idea to strip there.

There are other ways to send the message for those times when you'd rather not take your clothes off. For example, you can give him *verbal* clues.

Jane says:
"Here's a good idea: Use sneakily sexy words when you're talking to him."

You know, it's hard to switch channels, the remote button is so stiff. That reminds me—the other day I saw this amazing footage on TV—some giant thruster rockets blasting off. And they went into this warm tunnel...

This kind of sneakily sexy conversation should get his rockets revved!

Jane says:

"And you can get even more sneaky . . ."

Here's an example of what Jane is talking about. Say the following—and don't be surprised if you don't get a chance to say another word!

Sample script:

"I want to get the microwave fixed since I have noticed it doesn't get the coffee hot enough. In that dirty old box over there, there should be a monkey wrench. I'd love it if you could fix the microwave with it, but if you can't, I'll get on it myself. Be careful not to make a mess on the floor, all right? Now. . . let's get started!"

All right, so maybe you're thinking, "Why would talking about a microwave lead to passionate sex?" Let's look a little more closely at this paragraph—or, rather, at a certain word PATTERN in here.

The pattern 1, 2, 3, 10, 17, 21, 30, 33, 41, 45, 49, 60, 61, 63, and 64 immediately springs to mind. This simple pattern gives you the placement of *special key words* that deliver a hidden message to his boy brain.

Sample script with key words highlighted:

I want to get the microwave fixed since I **have** noticed it doesn't get the coffee **hot** enough. In that **dirty** old box over there, there should be a **monkey** wrench. I'd **love** it if you could fix the microwave **with** it, but if **you** can't, I'll get **on** it myself. Be careful not to make a mess on **the floor**, all **right**? **Now** . . . let's get started!

Okay, now take those key words and put them together into a sentence: "I want to have . . ." and so on.

Jane says:

"Get the message? He sure will!"

Okay, so we've looked at how you can signal that you want sex. How about the signals *he* might be sending *you?* These tend to be pretty easy to figure out . . .

Key Phrases That Indicate That He Wants Sex

When he says . . .	He means . . .
"How about a little kiss?"	"I want to have sex."
"What's for dinner?"	"I want to have sex."
"I like that dress."	"I want to have sex."
"Boy, it was hot today."	"I want to have sex."
"Where's the remote?"	"I want to have sex—after I find the remote."
"Wanna go to the movies?"	"I want to have sex."
"Have you lost weight?"	"I definitely want to have sex."

Problem Boys

In your dating career, you will meet different kinds of boys.

Some of them will
be studs.

STUD

But many of them
will be . . . duds.

DUD

Here's a rundown of some of the duds to watch out for—
or, as Jane likes to call them . . .

Dangerous Dicks.

Jane's Special Secret #14:
Watch out for "Bug Boys."

If he's starting to bug you, there might be a VERY good reason!

Modern scientists (especially insect scientists called "entomologists") have discovered a fascinating fact: Some annoying boys are JUST LIKE BUGS.

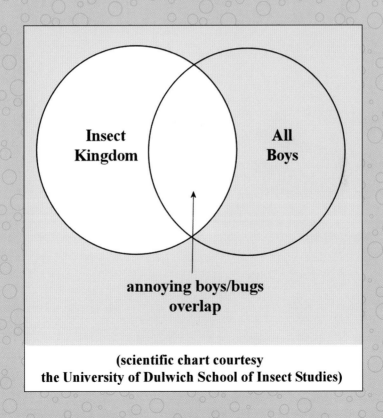

annoying boys/bugs
overlap

(scientific chart courtesy
the University of Dulwich School of Insect Studies)

They share the same characteristics. They share the same irritating habits. They both, well, bug you!

Just like you don't want a bug in your kitchen, you sure don't want a bug in your bed, do you?

Jane says:

"Face it, girls—sometimes when it comes to the guy in your life, it's time to get out the fly swatter!"

Jane adds:

"Or bug spray!"

But how can you tell if that cute guy's annoying habits are just part of the usual male package—or if they're telling you that he's all BUG underneath?

Just as an entomologist (an insect scientist, remember?) classifies bugs and uses this information to exterminate them, *you* can classify boys and use this information to decide which boys should check into the dating roach motel.

With the help of several important female entomologists, Jane has devised a handy quiz. Not only will it help you determine whether your boy is a bug, it will tell you what KIND of bug you're dealing with!

 Jane says:
"This can be useful when figuring out whether to 'swat,' 'spray,' or 'step on and crush' him."

So get your pencils ready and put your thinking caps on. You're about to find out . . .

is he a Man Roach?!?
Or worse.

JANE'S HELPFUL QUIZ: WHAT KIND OF BUG IS HE?

(1) You're with him in a restaurant. He:

    (a) asks the waiter for recommendations.

    (b) orders the special of the day in fluent French.

    (c) eats all of your leftovers—including crumbs, gristle, and that piece of meat you spit out because it was too tough.

If you answered "C" . . . a Man Roach might be in your presence.

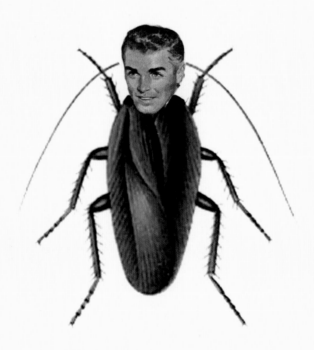

Man Roach Identifying Characteristics:

- Wonderful to have around in a post–nuclear war environment, but that's about it.
- Used to belong to frat. Still acts as if he does.
- Has nickname like Booger. Still answers to it.
- Drug of choice: beer (domestic; cheapest).
- Watches all sports all the time. If unable to watch pro sports, will watch gripping televised bowling championship rerun from 1976.
- Wears gray-green underwear (formerly white).
- Sex with him: sloppy.

(2) When he has free time, he likes to:

(a) go to the gym and work out.

(b) watch TV.

(c) "pollinate" other girls.

If you answered "C" . . . he may be a Bee.

Bee Boy Identifying Characteristics:

- Loves to spread that "pollen" around. So if you don't mind knowing that he's seeing a lot of other "stamens" (or even "pistils"), he may be okay for you.
- Often in the entertainment industry and in the upper echelons of finance.
- Works hard—and plays harder.
- Drugs of choice: single-malt scotch, name-brand vodkas, French wine, cocaine (pharmaceutical grade).
- Permanently wired to the worldwide "hive."
- Manscaped.
- Sex with him: frequent.

(3) In terms of his body, he:

(a) has six-pack abs and pecs that won't quit.

(b) is average-looking; not bad but not great.

(c) is a lump of blobby, pale, pulsating flesh whose idea of exercise is rolling over on the couch.

If you answered "C" . . . you probably have a Larva on your hands.

Larva Lad Identifying Characteristics:

- Mama's boy—often can be found living in Mom's basement or accepting monthly rent stipend (and frozen lasagna) from Mom.
- Expert at appealing to women's maternal instincts.
- (If employed) Works in family business or in low-level municipal position.
- Tends to talk incessantly about high school days.
- Preferred foods: soda (non-diet), chip-based foods, and mac and cheese.
- Drug of choice: marijuana.
- Sex with him: soft and cuddly. And damp.

(4) His personality can be summed up with the following quotation:

(a) "Eat, drink, and be merry!"

(b) "Seize the day!"

(c) "I don't have time for quotations. I've got work to do."

If you answered "C" . . . he may be an Ant.

Ant Boy Identifying Characteristics:

- Tends to be community banker, accountant, pharmacist, podiatrist, or dentist.
- Tends to talk too much about community banking, accounting, filling prescriptions, corns and bunions, or flossing.
- Excellent provider with well-stocked 401(k), retirement plan, etc.
- Tends to talk too much about well-stocked 401(k), retirement plan, etc.
- Watches CNBC, Fox News, and/or CNN.
- Talks too much about news as seen on CNBC, Fox News, and/or CNN.
- Drug of choice: none.
- Sex with him: limited.

Jane's Special Secret #14: A Real-Life Example

Chelsea's love life was bug-ridden. She was infested with wimpy men, boring men, limp men, and other undesirables. With Jane's help, she was able to identify and eradicate the bugs already in her life. Plus she learned how to spot bugs coming on to her at work, at the gym, at clubs.

The result? Chelsea has been bug-free for six months! And now she has met Ryan . . .

 Jane says:

"Don't settle! You deserve better than a bug, girlfriend!"

Chelsea Enjoys a Pest-Free Life

Jane's Special Secret #15:

**Perfect Boys can be duds, too.
Ask yourself: If he's perfect, why isn't he taken?
(There's usually a perfect reason . . .)**

Sometimes you meet the Boy of Your Dreams. He is everything you could hope for. He is handsome. He is successful. He is funny.

He has a great bod. And—best of all—he doesn't have a girlfriend!

You will say to yourself, "The search is over. I have met Mr. Perfect."

He invites you to go shopping with him to help him pick out a new fall outfit. He knows a *lot* about fashion. It is actually fun to talk with him about shoes! He really *is* perfect!

Then he invites you over to meet a friend and share a special brunch at his Chelsea apartment.

. . . Can you see where this is going? (If you can't figure it out, look at the next page.)

Mr. Perfect

Mr. Perfect &
His Mr. Perfect

You're right! The perfect man has his *own* perfect man!

 Jane says:

"Just because he has balls doesn't mean he wants to shoot a basket in your—or any other girl's—hoop!"

Jane's Special Secret #16:
Beware of the Disguised Dud!

Boys are a lot like advertising executives: They believe in the hard sell. What do advertising executives do? They sell things. Like soap. Or cars. Even if the soap doesn't clean that well, or the car doesn't drive that fast, advertising executives have to make believe they are worth buying. So they write "ads" or "commercials" that make the soap or the car sound a whole lot better than it really is.

Some boys do the same thing. Not with coffee, cars, or soap, but with THEMSELVES. They will tell you they are stronger than they really are, or richer, or smarter. They will make things up about themselves to impress you. This is called "the hard sell."

For example, a boy you met online e-mails his picture to you. Here it is:

Wow. He is so brooding and masculine. He looks hot. He also looks exciting and interesting. But don't get too excited. You may be a victim of *FALSE ADVERTISING*. You may be buying bad soap, so to speak. Or a slow car.

Why? Because here is what he *really* looks like:

Maybe it is just us, but he does not look hot. Or brooding. Or even that masculine . . . Yes. This Dick is a Disguised Dud.

Jane says:
"Don't judge a book by its cover . . . or a boy by his Photoshopped picture!"

Other times a boy will be like an *honest* ad executive. He will still advertise himself. He will still use the hard sell on you. He will be truthful. This is called "truth in advertising."

But he STILL might be a Dud in Disguise.

Want proof? Read the next horrifying real-life example!

Jane's Special Secret #16: A Real-Life Example

Carly liked "fast" boys. Brandon said he was a "fast" boy.

And Brandon seemed as fast as they come. He drove fast cars. He hung out with a fast crowd. He wore a motorcycle jacket.

But Carly's mom had always warned her about fast boys.

"They will break your heart," she said.

But Carly didn't care.

Carly slept with Brandon for the FIRST time tonight.

He was fast, all right. He lasted five minutes.

(Carly also slept with Brandon for the LAST time tonight.)

Jane says:

"Mom was right after all. Fast boys ARE bad news!"

Jane's Special Secret #17:
Finally, the Bad Boy problem.

Bad boys aren't always duds. They can be very exciting. But some bad boys are bad for you. (And some bad boys are good for you!) (And some good boys are bad for you!)

The trick is knowing how to spot the *good* bad boy and to avoid the *bad* bad boy and the bad *good* boy.

Let's start at the beginning. Even good girls have a little bit of bad girl inside of them. That is why so many good girls look at a bad boy and feel their knees get all rubbery, and their hearts go thumpathumpa, and their stomachs feel like they are filled with butterflies.

Bad boys are exciting. Dangerous. Mysterious. (Or, as the French say, "*mystérieux.*") Who doesn't get a little thrill when a bad boy asks you out?

Does this mean you should say yes? (Or, as the French say, "*Oui*"?)

That is a good question. It all depends . . .

Here is a table comparing:

(1) a bad boy who is bad for you,

(2) a bad boy who is good for you,

(3) a standard-issue good boy, and

(4) a good boy who is so sickeningly good, he is bad.

	Bad Bad Boy	Good Bad Boy	Good Boy	Bad Good Boy
untamed masculinity	X	X		
domesticated masculinity			X	
questionable masculinity				X
wears black nylon socks to bed				X
wears nylon stocking over head (when holding up store)	X			
asks you to wear black stockings and garter belt in bed		X		
tells cute jokes			X	
tells crude jokes	X			
tells funny, sometimes racy jokes		X		
tells clean, safe-for-the-whole-family jokes				X
looks devilishly handsome	X			
looks roguishly handsome		X		
looks handsomely clean-cut			X	
looks squeaky-clean				X
thinks Hells Angels are too wimpy	X			
beaten up frequently by teenagers who dress a lot like Hells Angels				X

	Bad Bad Boy	Good Bad Boy	Good Boy	Bad Good Boy
likes playing games (poker)			X	
likes playing games (strip poker)	X			
likes playing games (strip backgammon)		X		
likes playing games (parcheesi)				X
smells like good cologne			X	
smells like hot animal passion		X		
smells like sweat	X			
smells like nasal decongestant spray				X
gives you drugs (hard)	X			
gives you drugs (champagne)		X		
gives you drugs (allergy medication)				X
favorite film: *Lesbian Lovers Go Wild*	X			
favorite film: any chick flick you want to see			X	
favorite film: *Easy Rider*		X		
favorite film: the third *Star Trek* film (with the missing footage and Klingon subtitles)				X

As you can see, the bad bad boy is too bad. The bad good boy is too good. The good boy is okay. And the good bad boy is just right!

 Jane says:
"Just like porridge!"

Jane's Special Secret #17: A Real-Life Example

Good girl Brooke had been an item with good boy Brad ever since second grade.

Then she met Black Bart . . .

"Black Bart is a BAD BOY!" everyone warned her. "That means he is a BAD CHOICE!"

But Brooke wasn't that sure . . .

So she invited both Brad and Black Bart over for a snack. She could compare them head-to-head!

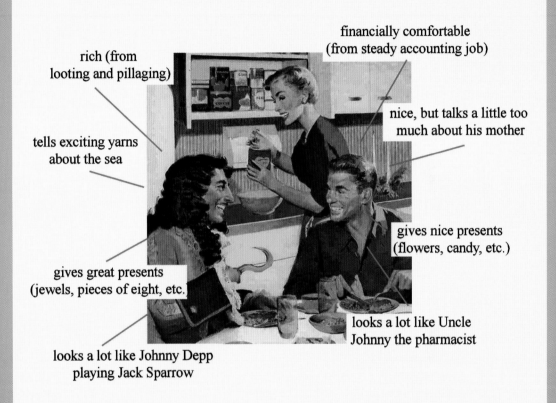

rich (from looting and pillaging)

financially comfortable (from steady accounting job)

tells exciting yarns about the sea

nice, but talks a little too much about his mother

gives great presents (jewels, pieces of eight, etc.

gives nice presents (flowers, candy, etc.)

looks a lot like Uncle Johnny the pharmacist

looks a lot like Johnny Depp playing Jack Sparrow

Look at the picture and tell us who YOU would choose.

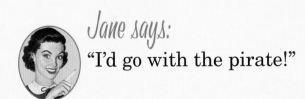

Jane says:
"I'd go with the pirate!"

Okay, so you've met a great boy. You've gone on several dates. You've had sex, or at least have enjoyed exploring each other's bodies in pleasurable ways. You like spending time together.

People think of you as a couple.

Yes. You are officially In a Relationship.

This means you are, in effect, on a "ship" of *relating*.

 Jane says:

"Get it? Relation. Ship. So you'd better learn how to be captain of a *seaworthy* (relation) ship. "

This section teaches you how to steer your ship around the whirlpools of unreasonable expectations, past the looming rocks of "taking things for granted," across the sandbars of sex problems, and into the port of Mutually Satisfactory Passion and Communication.

So let's get going—and anchors aweigh!

Jane's Special Secret #18:

If you have high expectations about his behavior in a relationship, you're on the wrong planet, sister . . .

You've heard the saying and it's all too true. Men ARE from Mars. Here is an interesting scientific fact: The gravity on Mars is 38 percent lower than gravity on Earth. This means that here on Earth you have to lower your expectations to the low Martian level of male behavior. Specifically, you should lower your expectations of boy behavior in a relationship by AT LEAST 38 percent.

Expect him to be clumsy. Expect him to make mistakes.

Expect him to think fart jokes are hysterically funny. Expect him to forget your birthday/anniversary/special holidays. Expect him to wear those horrible sneakers to your boss's cocktail party.

He can't help it, poor thing, since underneath that human male exterior lurks a . . . .

MAN FROM MARS!!!

What You See   What You Get

The problem is, no matter how many times you tell yourself to lower your expectations, it's awfully darn hard. You, a female, have high expectations. He, a male, has low expectations.

So what's a gal to do?

Short of being a lesbian, if you want a happy relationship, you *have* to learn to settle. Pushing him to meet your high standards will break him. And you don't want a broken boy, do you?

We think not.

Jane says:

"As I always say, don't forget my simple relationship equation: LE=HHRQ (lower expectations = higher happiness relationship quotient)."

That said, you do have the right to have certain minimum demands met. You don't want to over-lower your standards. This leads to that magic word "compromise."

Let us see how this works in real life. Following is a case study pulled from Jane's extensive files. (We have omitted the names to protect the privacy of the people involved.)

In it, you will see:

- a typical female ideal Valentine's Day;
- the corresponding low-quality typical male ideal Valentine's Day; and
- the all-too-typical *compromise* Valentine's Day.

JANE'S CASE STUDY

#1: Her Ideal Valentine's Day

7:30 A.M.: Wakes up. Finds Valentine card and small chocolate heart on pillow. Card reads: "I've finally found the only one for me. I love you more than I can ever say."

8:00 A.M.: Finds love poem taped to coffee machine.

10:00 A.M.: Large box containing a dozen long-stemmed red roses delivered to her desk at work. Coworkers "ooh" and "ahh."

12:30 P.M.: Small box containing tasteful but gorgeous piece of jewelry delivered to her desk at work. Coworkers openly envious.

5:00 P.M.: He's waiting in office lobby; escorts her to that romantic restaurant she's been dying to go to.

6:00 P.M.: Have drinks, then dinner (and imported champagne) at corner table that takes months to get reservation for. Feeds her strawberries dipped in chocolate. Kisses her fingers. Tells her he has never been this happy.

8:00 P.M.: Home to rose-petal-strewn bed. Passionate, caring, tender sex with relationship conversation afterward.

(She thinks he seems close to popping the question!)

11:00 P.M.: Blissful, sated sleep

#2: His Ideal Valentine's Day

7:30 A.M.: Wakes up.

8:00 A.M.: Showers, goes to work.

10:00 A.M.: Working. Praised by boss. Coworkers "ooh" and "ahh."

12:30 P.M.: Wins office basketball pool. Coworkers openly envious.

5:00 P.M.: Goes out for a few brews with the boys. Bartender impressed by basketball knowledge.

6:00 P.M.: Comes home. Eats. Girlfriend serves dinner wearing slutty lingerie and heels. Because it's Valentine's Day, have wine instead of beer. Wild sex on kitchen floor.

8:00 P.M.: Watches sports on TV.

9:10 P.M.: Quickie sex during commercial.

9:13 P.M.: Back to TV sports. Switches over to beer. Snacks.

11:00 P.M.: Wild sex in bed. (Because it's Valentine's Day, she says, "Whatever you want.") Rolls over and goes to sleep. (Because it's Valentine's Day, no need for postsex conversation.)

#3: The Actual Valentine's Day

7:30 A.M.: Both wake up.

8:00 A.M.: On way to work, he notices people carrying red boxes around. Realizes "Oh my God, it's Valentine's Day."

10:00 A.M.: He rushes to office, asks secretary for phone number of Dial-a-Teddy, calls, and gets special "rush order," which they promise will arrive at her office by 12:30.

12:30 P.M.: Calls her at office; asks if she likes teddy. What teddy? He says, "Oh, fuck," and hangs up.

12:32 P.M.: He calls Dial-a-Teddy, screams, threatens.

12:55 P.M.: Package delivered to her desk—leather-clad teddy bear with card saying "Happy Valentine's Day to My Dream Guy." Confused. Coworkers "ooh" and "ahh" over stupidity of boyfriend. They wonder about sex life (open-ass leather chaps?) and boyfriend (dream guy?).

5:00 P.M.: He's waiting in office lobby with unnaturally colored carnations bought at corner deli; escorts her to that romantic restaurant she's been dying to go to. Can't get in without reservations.

6:00 P.M.: Have drinks at next-door bar. Bartender impressed with his basketball knowledge. Finally decide to go out for Chinese. At Chinese restaurant, she hands him Valentine's card. He gets pale. Excuses himself to go to bathroom.

Returns in twenty minutes with non-heart-shaped box of sugar-free chocolates especially for diabetics (she is not diabetic. Also, box is dented) and Valentine's card in Spanish. Neither of them speaks Spanish. (Because it's Valentine's Day, last card left in store.) *It's the thought that counts,* both think.

8:00 P.M.: Home. Nice, normal sex with TV afterward.

11:00 P.M.: Sleep.

Case study analysis:

You will note that the actual Valentine's Day is pretty dreary. Neither the boy nor the girl has a wonderful time. And they both wind up with mediocre Chinese food.

This is called . . . *the wonderful compromise of love.*

Jane says:

The beauty of all this is that NEITHER was particularly thrilled about how the day turned out. And that's the whole point—they're *sharing*. Sharing mediocrity! Together!

Jane's Special Secret #19:

Sometimes a boy just isn't able to share his "manliness" with you. But don't throw in the towel! (So to speak.)

This is another case where the "compromise of love" is important. You see, there's going to be a time when a boy is going to let you down. Literally.

Boys are far from perfect. You know that. The world knows that. And sometimes their parts don't work as perfectly as either of you would like.

It is very tempting to leave your malfunctioning Dick and find a new, more vigorous one. You might start eyeing the cute guy on the StairMaster. Or that stud fireman you pass on the way to yoga class as he's rolling out his hose.

Jane says:
"My advice is simple: Don't do it! 'Compromise of love,' remember?"

Your compromise here is being *patient* and *caring*. He needs you to "pump up" his confidence . . . and more! Remind yourself of the reasons you went out with him in the first place. (Besides that one.) He is *not* a one-trick pony.

This is not the time to focus on this one failure. There are other things you love about him. You know he's good for you.

You know your relationship has been working. So be patient and don't trade him in for someone new.

Besides, who knows? That fireman with the hose might have his own problems . . .

 Jane says:
"Remember, a Dick in the hand is worth two in the bush!"

Jane's Special Secret #19: A Real-Life Example

It had been a hard time for Kim and Aaron. Well, maybe "hard" is the wrong word . . .

Aaron wasn't shooting as well as he usually did. He had lost confidence in himself. He just couldn't do it.

"I am so embarrassed," he told Kim.

But Kim was a smart girl. She didn't get upset. She didn't act unfulfilled. She didn't pout. She thought about Jane's advice and knew how to act.

"Don't worry," she told him. "We can work this out together. In the meantime, we can enjoy other things."

Now take a look at the target. . .

Two bull's-eyes! Nice shooting, Aaron!
"You betcha!" says the very satisfied Kim.

Jane's Special Secret #20:

Sometimes it's not your DICK that's limp, it's the entire relationship.

This is the time for you to do some serious assessment.

The first thing you have to ask yourself: Is your Relation Ship foundering on the rocks? What's wrong? Is it you? Or is it him? In other words, are you a bored Captain? Or is he a bored Crew?

Take these scientifically designed diagnostic tests and find out.

Test 1: Are YOU bored with him?

(1) When he kisses you, you:
   (a) get tingles up and down your spine.
   (b) feel nice and warm.
   (c) think about the cold, vast, empty vacuum of outer space and wonder whether life has any meaning, then think about vacuuming the living room.

(2) You're planning your summer vacation. You:
    (a) surprise him with an all-expenses-paid trip to that romantic resort in St. Barts.
    (b) arrange for you both to chip in for a trip to that romantic resort in St. Bart's.
    (c) sneak off by yourself to that romantic resort in St. Bart's.

(3) You're having a stay-in night—just you two, a bottle of wine, and that movie you wanted to see. What do you do?
    (a) You put on your silk push-up bra with matching panties and garter belt, cuddle up, and start to watch movie . . . then get into some hot and heavy sex.
    (b) You cuddle up on the couch and watch the movie.
    (c) You decide it's the perfect time to Ped-Egg those pesky thick calluses on your heels.

(4) Someone asks you to describe the man in your life. You describe him as a lot like:
    (a) that hot guy in that new romantic comedy.
    (b) the guy next door.
    (c) Donald Duck.

If you answered "C" to each question, yes, you are bored with him.

Jane says:

"There's only one solution. Dump him. Now."

Jane adds:

"Well, if he has a lot of money, ask yourself: Is he REALLY that boring? (Ha ha! Just joking.) (I think . . .)"

Test 2: Is HE bored with you?

(1) For Valentine's Day, he gives you:

    (a) expensive jewelry and/or expensive lingerie.

    (b) flowers and/or luscious chocolates.

    (c) salted mixed nuts (over 50 percent peanuts).

(2) During foreplay (or heavy petting sessions), he:

    (a) calls you by your pet name.

    (b) calls you by your real name.

    (c) has forgotten your name.

(3) During sex, he:
- (a) talks dirty.
- (b) is silent, but moans.
- (c) falls asleep.

(4) After sex, he:
- (a) cuddles you.
- (b) kisses you good night.
- (c) stays asleep.

If you answered "C" to each question, yes, he is bored with you.

 Jane says:
"Remember: if he's snoring, you're boring!"

But this time there IS a solution: You have to focus on Revitalizing Your Dick!

Jane's Special Secret #21:

There are a number of things you can do to bring life back into your relationship and, yes, Revitalize Your Dick. (Or Tom. Or Harry.)

Yes, you can put the "oomph" back into your relationship.

All it takes is a little thought, a little creativity, and a whole lotta love!

Good communication is a must. You have to *communicate* your love for him. For example, why not call him at work every half hour, just to say "I love you"? It's guaranteed to get his attention!

"And if he gets fired for being on the phone too much, he'll have even more time to share with you!"

Another important revitalization tool: compliments.

Praise your boyfriend as much as possible. You don't have to lie, though. Tell the truth—but in a nice way. For example, during sex, instead of getting peeved because he's too fast, focus on his *positives*. You might say something like: "You know, I think you lasted a whole minute longer than usual!" He'll feel great! And maybe next time, you'll get *another* extra minute to "get there."

And be more creative when it comes to sex. You don't have to have sex just in the bedroom. Try other places—the great outdoors, male locker rooms, the post office . . .

One hot idea: Show up at his office, nude, under a raincoat—in front of his colleagues! They'll be jealous, all right!

Then have sex on his desk! We bet he'll remember that day for sure!

Jane says:

"And if he gets fired for having sex at work, he'll have even more time to have sex with you!"

Speaking of creative, there's always role-playing to add spice to your love life: Doctor and nurse, Antony and Cleopatra, Romeo and Juliet, pilot and flight attendant, Albert Einstein and Marie Curie . . . The possibilities are endless!

Try any of these ideas—or come up with some of your own—and your relationship will be back on course. Ahoy, Captain! Full steam ahead!

Jane's Special Secret #21: A Real-Life Example

Don and Dana's relationship had hit the deadly doldrums.

They were b-o-r-e-d.

Now, thanks to Jane, they are exploring the magical world of role-playing to revitalize things.

Sometimes Don is the traffic cop who has pulled Dana over. Other times, Dana is the strict schoolteacher and Don is the bad, bad boy. But Don likes it best when he becomes his childhood hero, Don Diego de la Vega—better known as . . . Zorro!

In fact, Don likes playing Zorro so much, he is revitalizing their relationship every chance he gets!

"Sometimes I wish I had never bought him those damn tights," says Dana.

Jane's Special Secret #22
Sometimes you just have to prune your Dick.

Sadly, there may come a time when you face relationship problems that just won't go away and can't be solved. These are the problems that keep on growing and eventually choke the "garden of love" (which is located on the *deck* of your Relation Ship).

Confused? So are we. But no matter.

The point is that if the "garden of love" you used to share is dead, there is only one solution: Instead of trying to prune those weeds to get things growing again, you've got to cut your losses—and, yes, cut off that Dick.

Ouch! It can be painful—but sometimes it just has to be done. Chopping off, lopping off, or otherwise pruning that bad Dick in your life . . .

Jane says:

"Don't be a lazy gardener! Sharpen up those 'relationship pruning shears' and cut, cut, cut!"

How can you be a good "gardener"? Here are a few of Jane's most successful Relationship Pruning Tips.

- ***Don't get angry.*** That makes HIM get angry, too—and makes the whole break-up process unpleasant. This is why words like "asshole," "pig," and "dickwad" are not advised.

- ***Along these lines, this is not the time to insult him.*** For example, avoid references to small baby gherkins, limp egg noodles, and so forth.

- ***Be specific and honest.*** If he asks, let him know why you think it's not working. But do try to keep it nice. For example, avoid references to small baby gherkins, limp egg noodles, and so forth.

Keep it simple, sweetie! Boys often aren't that good with words anyway. It's best to use easy-to-understand words (one syllable is best) so the idea that you are breaking up with him can get into his boy brain.

Keep your emotions in check. Laughing hysterically when he asks if you can give it another chance is inappropriate.

Choose the right place and time to break up with him. Preferably private and preferably not a special occasion.

His birthday? Bad. Valentine's Day? Bad. Yankee Stadium public address system? Bad.

Jane's Final—and Most Important—Special Secret:

**Never forget—*there is someone for everyone.*
There is a Dick out there for each and every girl.**

As Winston Churchill, the British prime minister, once said: "Never give in. Never give in. Never, never, never, never."

He actually was talking about a war (World War II). But he could just as well have been talking about finding a boy—the *right* boy!

Jane says:

"You want to hear something interesting? Churchill won his war. Just like you can win your boy!"

Go get 'em, girlfriend!

Yes, your perfect match is waiting somewhere out there for you . . .

Sure, it might take some time and you'll be worrying, "Will I ever meet the right guy?" . . .

Hildy's main squeeze

But you will!

And, sure, you'll probably kiss so many frogs, you'll think you'll never find your prince . . .

But you will!

And sometimes you might think that you'll never meet a boy who has the same interests, habits, hobbies, obsessive-compulsive traits, outlook on life, or sense of humor . . .

But you will!

Jane found her Dick.

Will you find yours?

 Jane says:
"Yes, you bet you will!"